We are
GIRLS

D1080814

Olivia
and the
Outstanding Fair

BONNEY
PRESS

Published by Bonney Press,
an imprint of Hinkler Books Pty Ltd 2019
45–55 Fairchild Street
Heatherton Victoria 3202 Australia
www.hinkler.com

BONNEY
PRESS

Story by Katie Hewat
Biographies by Debra Thomas
Illustrations by Kayla Harren

Editorial: Emily Murray and Sam Kiley
Design: Bianca Zuccolo
Publishing Manager: Jennifer Bilos
Prepress: Splitting Image

ISBN: 978 1 4889 7605 6

Printed and bound in China

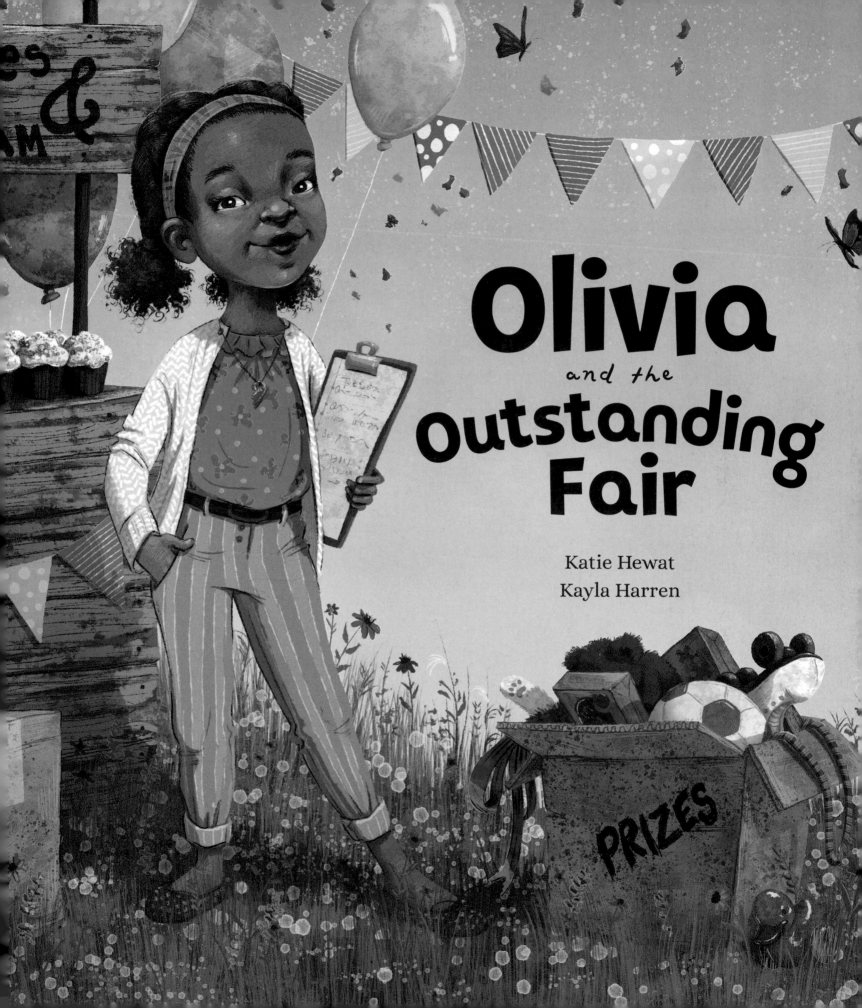

Olivia
and the
Outstanding
Fair

Katie Hewat

Kayla Harren

PRIZES

I'm a leader, a planner, a friend through and through;
I love helping others to do good things, too.

I like using my strengths to help people out;
being strong and supportive is what I'm about!

But I'm facing a challenge – this will be no breeze:
I've heard some sad news from my friend overseas.

In her letter it says that her school is in trouble;
they need help buying books, quick smart, on the double!

I visit my teacher and tell her my plan.
We'll hold a school fair and raise what we can.

My friend loves to learn just as much as I do.
I'll raise funds for her and the other kids, too!

I gather up friends to aid in the planning.
I'll need help setting up and the stalls will need manning.

I'm eager to tell my friends what can be done
if we all lend a hand and we all work as one.

We're at our school early on the day of the fair.
We're busy as bees, working hard to prepare.

I asked Adam and Deb to bake cupcakes to sell –
they offered to make us some ice-cream as well!

I've called local shops and asked for support
and welcomed donations of every sort!

We're having a raffle with lots of cool prizes: vouchers and hampers and toys of all sizes!

I decided to run a second-hand store
and asked kids to bring things they don't need any more.

We have books and clothes and some roller skates,
and Ms Jones' bike that she kindly donates.

I've rented a castle that's packed to the brim
and handed the reins to Sarah and Tim.

We're finally ready, exhausted but proud,
we open the gates and in floods the crowd!

People are laughing and having a ball
        and business is booming at every stall.
We play lots of games and eat ice-cream, too.
        This fair is such fun – there is so much to do!

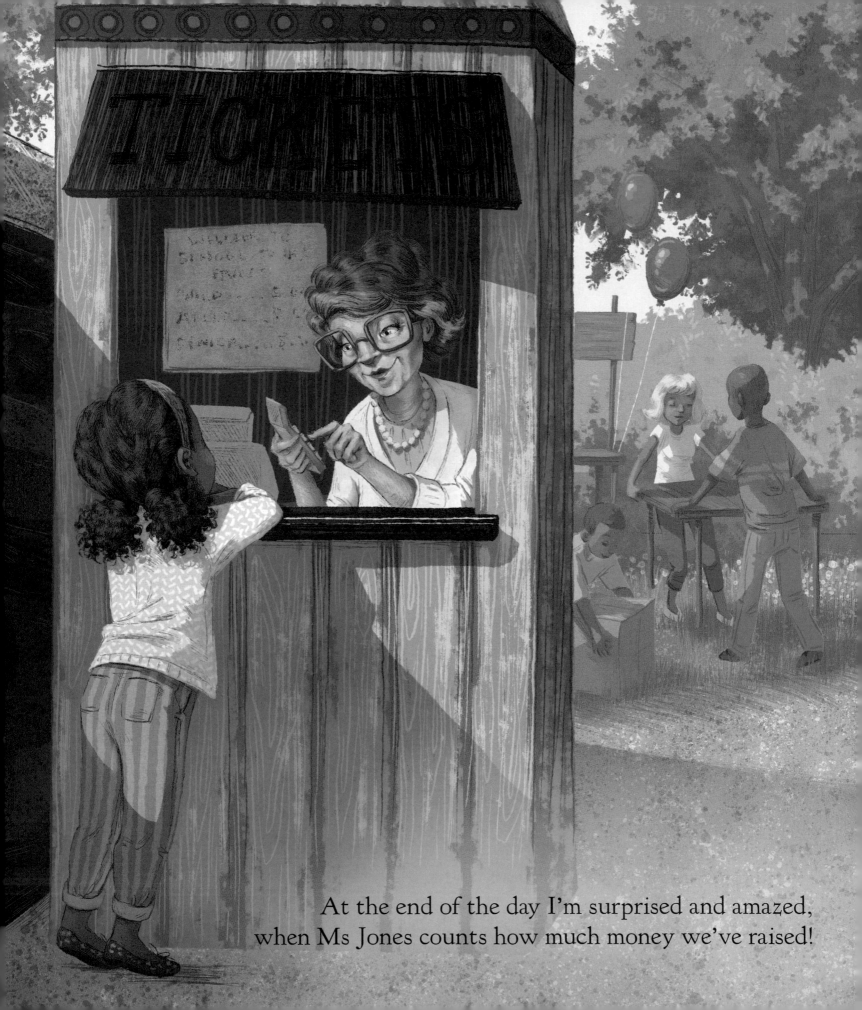

At the end of the day I'm surprised and amazed,
when Ms Jones counts how much money we've raised!

I'm over the moon when I see that it looks
like we can donate so much more than just books.

A week or so later, I'm thrilled to learn that my friend's school is calling on video chat!

For the very first time, I can see her face;

it almost feels like we are in the same place.

Her teacher waves hi and says she's delighted,
then shows me the things our donation provided.

I speak with my friend. We have a good chat!
Her school's so much better – more fun in fact.

I know in my heart, as our conversation ends,
there's no greater reward than supporting one's friends.

I knew it would happen; I knew I could do it!

I'll never give up once I set my mind to it.

The Women Who Inspired Olivia

Olivia immediately launched into action when she had a friend in need. By raising enough money to buy new books for her pen pal's school, Olivia improved the quality of both her friend's education and that of her fellow students. The world is filled with so many amazing women who support others and improve countless lives in many different ways. Here are 12 women we love; women who never gave up trying to help others despite the difficulty – and very often the risk – that it involved.

Florence Nightingale

*'I attribute my success to this –
I never gave or took any excuse.'*

12 May 1820 – 13 August 1910
ITALY

Florence was a nurse and mathematical genius. While treating wounded soldiers during the Crimean war, Florence used her remarkable mathematical ability to gather statistics proving that most soldiers died not of their war wounds, but from poor treatment. With this data, Florence garnered the attention of Queen Victoria. Her reforms changed health care around the world. Florence later trained nurses to help those who couldn't afford care and improved the quality of training for midwives to reduce the number of women dying in childbirth. In 1860, she established the first nursing school that focused on scientific treatment and was the first woman awarded the Order of Merit in 1907.

Vida Goldstein

'I know too much from [observing] how the poor and working classes live to be satisfied with a system which makes their lives one unceasing round of toil, deprivation and anxiety.'

13 April 1869 – 15 August 1949
AUSTRALIA

As a child, Vida worked alongside her mother Isabella to help support women and girls in poor Melbourne communities. These women's struggles stuck with Vida, and in 1899 she became the head of the Victorian women's movement. Many of Vida's campaigns were widely successful, and she led the revolution to get women the vote in Australia. In 1903, Vida became one of the first women to stand for election to federal parliament. Although she was unsuccessful, she paved the way for other women to enter politics.

Louisa May Alcott

*'I like to help women help themselves...
Whatever we can do and do well we have a right to, and I don't think any one will deny us.'*

29 November 1832 – 6 March 1888
UNITED STATES

Louisa's most famous novel, *Little Women*, showcased the March sisters as bold, smart, powerful women who could chart their own course in life. Just like the characters in *Little Women*, at a young age Louisa worked to support her family through their financial difficulties. As she got older and her writing became more successful, she used her voice to support others, including fighting for women's right to vote and working on campaigns to end slavery.

Helen Keller

'I long to accomplish a great and noble task, but it is my chief duty to accomplish small tasks as if they were great and noble.'

27 June 1880 – 1 June 1968
UNITED STATES

At 19 months old, Helen contracted an unknown disease that left her deaf and blind. At the age of 6 she was referred to the Perkins Institution for the Blind in Boston, where she met her teacher, Anne Sullivan, who taught her to communicate more effectively. After graduating from Harvard University in 1900, Helen became an advocate for various social causes, in particular for those living with disabilities. She has received countless accolades for her contributions, including being elected into the Women's Hall of Fame in 1965.

Gabi Hollows

'I believe that helping people was the right way to be. And you just gave someone else a hand up [and] they'll come back and help you if you need it.'

21 MAY 1953 –
AUSTRALIA

Gabi (then Gabrielle Beryl O'Sullivan) had eye surgery when she was just three years old. Wanting to help others see better, Gabi went on to become an orthoptist. After meeting ophthalmologist Fred Hollows during her training, they began travelling across Australia to provide treatment for preventable blindness in remote Indigenous communities. Fred and Gabi married in 1980 and continued their work across the globe. After Fred died in 1993, Gabi continued as Founding Director at the Fred Hollows Foundation, working to prevent and treat blindness. Gabi received the Advance Australia Award for Community Service in 2013.

Leymah Gbowee

'I will not stop ranting until my mission of equality of all girls is achieved.'

1 FEBRUARY 1972 –
LIBERIA

Leymah became a social worker during the First Liberian Civil War, helping ex-child soldiers deal with trauma. Through her work, Leymah began to believe that women could change the course of the violence she had witnessed. In 2002, she began leading a non-violent women's movement, putting pressure on the President to engage in peace talks to end the Second Liberian Civil War. This movement was instrumental in ending the fourteen-year war and led to a period of peace that saw the election of Africa's first female President, Ellen Johnson Sirleaf. Leymah was awarded the 2011 Nobel Peace Prize for her work in transforming the lives of countless African women.

Rigoberta Menchú Tum

'I am like a drop of water on a rock. After drip, drip, dripping in the same place, I begin to leave a mark... in many people's hearts.'

9 JANUARY 1959 –
GUATEMALA

As a teenager, Rigoberta became involved with the women's rights movement. After her family were murdered for their work in advancing Indian peasant rights, she became more active in her advocacy and became involved in protests and demonstrations against military oppression. In 1981, Rigoberta was forced to flee from Guatemala to Mexico. She has continued her work and is renowned for her advocacy in bringing different cultures together peacefully – and in 1992 she was awarded the Nobel Peace Prize.

Malala Yousafzai

'I raise up my voice – not so I can shout but so that those without a voice can be heard... we cannot succeed when half of us are held back.'

12 JULY 1997 –
PAKISTAN

Malala began speaking about her experience living under the Taliban at only 11 years old, blogging for the BBC. When she began receiving international attention for her work to ensure all girls could access their right to an education, the Taliban retaliated. Sending a masked gunman after her, Malala was shot in the head and critically injured. After a long recovery, Malala became an advocate for the educational rights of girls all over the world. Launching a series of successful campaigns and organisations, Malala was a co-recipient of the Nobel Peace Prize in 2014.